Thibaud **VILLANOVA**

GASTRONO GEEK

CULT TV SERIES

Mathilde **BOURGE**

PHOTOGRAPHS
Nicolas **LOBBESTAËL**

PHOTO STYLING
Soizic **CHOMEL DE VARAGNES**

EDITORIAL PACKAGING
GASTRONOGEEK

ILLUSTRATIONS
Bérengère **DEMONCY**

TITAN BOOKS

Welcome to our new geek cookbook!

If you're not familiar with the concept, Gastronogeek® serves as a bridge between two passions: gastronomy and the imaginative realms of geek and popular culture.

You might wonder, "Wouldn't geeks just stick to a chips-pizza-soda diet, slumped in front of their TV or computer screen?" Well, it's time to dispel that old cliché...

Since 2014, Gastronogeek® has been my response to a simple question: If chefs today derive inspiration from childhood memories or flavors discovered during their travels to craft new dishes, why can't I draw inspiration from references ingrained in me since childhood? These references span from pop cultural icons in fantasy literature or genre cinema to video games and TV series.

Starting with a cookbook that offered complete menus surrounding 15 representative references of geek culture—from *Harry Potter* to *Doctor Who*, via *The Lord of the Rings* and *Superman*—followed by a *Book of Potions* the subsequent year, and culminating in THE official Star Wars™ cookbook, what you now hold in your hands is a geek cookbook dedicated to over thirty cult series!

How much of my life have I spent immersed in the adventures of Kirk and Spock, Sam Beckett, the Doctor, Buffy Summers, and Colonel O'Neill? How many times have I envisioned wielding a Masamune sword like Duncan MacLeod, born 400 years ago in the Scottish Highlands, or piloting a Viper Mark II alongside Starbuck and Apollo? How often have I dreamt of sharing the daily lives of the Halliwell sisters, combating demons with spells and mystical powers? If I can't step through the screen, these pages serve as my culinary homage to them.

Slightly less geeky than its predecessors yet even more generous, this new installment in the Gastronogeek® saga delves into iconic pop culture references like *Sherlock*, *Breaking Bad*, *Vikings*, and *Hannibal*, each taking me on a journey as captivating as their more imaginative counterparts. To delight all culinary enthusiasts, I aimed for this book to honor the principles set in my previous works: creating recipes accessible to beginners and dedicated cooks alike, all while respecting the essence of the references cooked up within these pages.

I sincerely hope you embark on this new culinary adventure aboard the Gastronogeek® ship and find enjoyment in my humble tribute to these remarkable television worlds.

Cook long and prosper,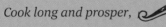

Thibaud Villanova

GASTRONO GEEK CULT TV SERIES

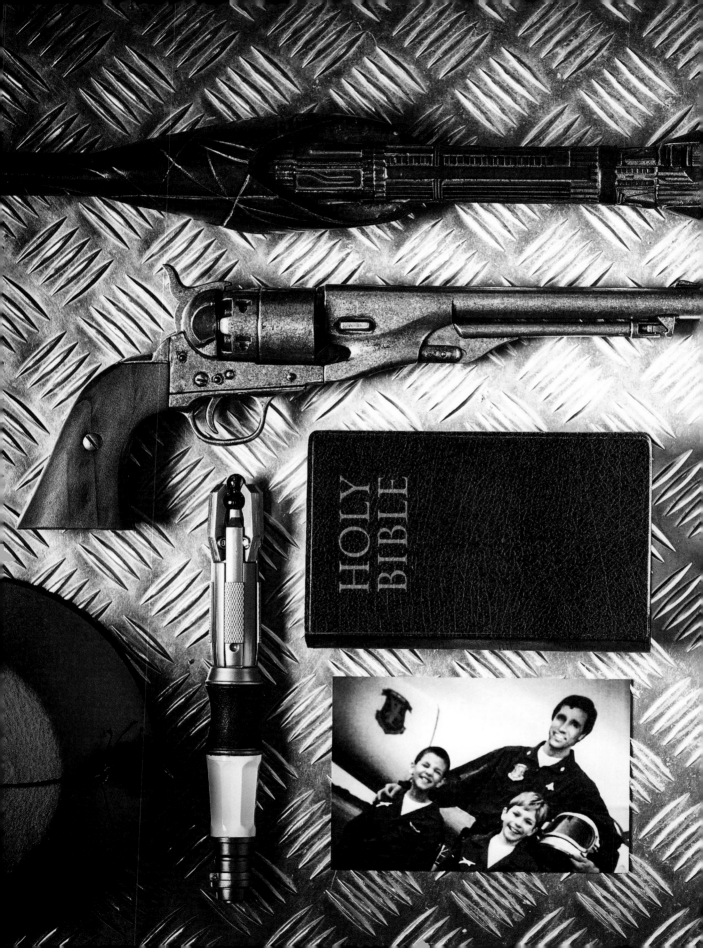

U.S.S. ENTERPRISE

STARFLEET REGISTRY NCC–1701-A
SAN FRANCISCO FLEET YARDS, EARTH
COMMISSIONED: STARDATE 8442.5
SECOND STARSHIP TO BEAR THE NAME

"...to boldly go where no man has gone before."

TO INFINITY AND BEYOND

Serves **4** - Preparation Time: **15 MIN** - Cooking time: **35 MIN**

It is widely acknowledged within Starfleet that plomeek soup holds a special place as a Vulcan favorite. Traditionally consumed in the morning, this soup is crafted from plomeek, a root vegetable native to Spock's home planet. Given the occasional difficulty in sourcing this ingredient, here is an adaptation of the recipe to easily prepare it on good old Earth.

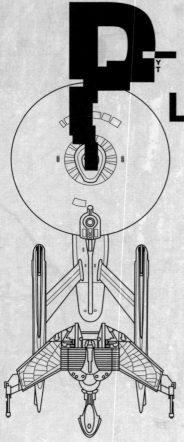

PLOMEEK SOUP
MORNING VEGETABLE SOUP

Start by preparing the vegetables. Peel and finely chop the onion. Finely chop the leeks. Peel the carrots and cut them into 1 cm cubes (mirepoix). Peel the parsnips and cut them into small 2 mm cubes (brunoise). Peel the sweet potato and cut it into 1 cm cubes (mirepoix). Coarsely chop the beetroot.

In a casserole dish, drizzle olive oil and add the butter, heating over medium heat. Add the chopped onion, leeks, and carrots. Cook for 5 minutes, then add the parsnip and sweet potato cubes. Fry for an additional 2 minutes and season to taste. Pour in the vegetable stock and simmer, covered, at a gentle boil for 25 minutes.

Remove the pot from the heat. With an immersion blender, blend the mixture for 2 minutes until it reaches a smooth consistency. Add the beetroot and blend for another 2 minutes to mix it thoroughly into the soup. And there you have it— plomeek soup is almost ready!

Serving suggestions: Serve this soup for dinner, accompanied by a small spoonful of fromage frais and a sprinkle of fresh parsley. This dish is known to bring energy, vitality, and wishes for long life and prosperity. Considering its ingredients, there's one person who would say it's... logical.

LEVEL:
APPRENTICE COOK

INGREDIENTS

1 large yellow onion
3 leek whites
2 carrots
1 parsnip
1 sweet potato
1 cooked beetroot
Olive oil
3 ½ tbsp (50 g) butter
2 ½ cups (600 ml) vegetable stock (see page 94)
Salt
Pepper
4 tsp. fresh cheese
Fresh parsley

For **4 BOWLS** - Preparation time: **20 MIN** - Cooking time: **15 MIN** (BOIL) + **1 MIN** (NOODLES)

Eating nothing but noodles and seaweed could drive some people mad. What would drive you crazy would be not eating at all, when you have survived an onslaught of those pesky toasters for the umpteenth time. Here is how to make a bowl of noodles fit for a starship commander!

ALGAE RATION

SOBA, MISO AND LOTUS ROOT

← Start by preparing the noodles: pour the buckwheat flour, wheat flour and matcha tea into a mixing bowl. Mix and make a well. Pour 50 ml of water into the well and knead. Gradually add the rest of the water until you obtain a smooth dough.

← Flour a work surface, roll out the dough into a rectangular block 2 mm thick. Flour it very lightly so that it doesn't stick and, using a paring knife, cut very thin strips of dough. Set aside. Your fresh noodles are ready to cook.

← For the regenerating broth: slice the lemongrass stalks lengthwise. Peel the lotus root and cut into thin slices. Pour the water and barley miso into a saucepan. Bring to the boil, then add the lemongrass and leave to infuse for 10 minutes, keeping it boiling. Remove the lemongrass and add the lotus, kikurage, wakame and edamame. Boil for 3 minutes. The broth is now ready; simmer over a low heat while you cook the noodles.

← Bring a pan of lightly salted water to the boil and immerse the noodles in it for 1 minute before draining them and running them under cold water for a few seconds.

To serve, place a portion of noodles in 4 bowls, pour over the broth and vegetables. Taste and take a few moments with your XO to prepare for the next PRL jump.

LEVEL:
XO

INGREDIENTS

FOR SOBA NOODLES
*1 ½ cups (200 g)
buckwheat flour
¾ cups (100 g) wheat flour
½ tsp. matcha tea
½ cup (150 ml) room-
temperature water*

FOR THE BROTH
*2 stalks lemongrass
½ cup (100 g) lotus root
4 cups (1 l) water
1 tbsp. barley miso
4 pinches dried kikurage
(black mushroom)
4 pinches wakame (seaweed)
2 ½ tbsp (20 g) edamame*

Serves **6** - Preparation time: **15 MIN** - Cooking time: **40 MIN**

Every Jaffa warrior was once a child, and it's well known that the children of Chulak love Satta cakes: Rya'c, the son of Drey'auc and Teal'c, has never made a secret of it. Here's how the Tau'ri make this cake.

SATTA CAKE
DATE, APPLE, AND HAZELNUT CAKE

← Preheat your oven to 180°C (gas mark 6).

← Begin by preparing the fruit. Remove the pits and chop the dates. Peel, core, and dice the apples into 2 mm cubes. Crush the hazelnuts and pistachios. Set them aside for a few moments, then proceed to prepare the cake mixture.

← In a mixing bowl, place the butter and sugar. Whisk vigorously until the mixture whitens. Gradually whisk in the eggs, one at a time. Add the cream, followed by the flour, cornstarch, hazelnut powder, and baking powder. Mix until you achieve a thick, homogeneous cream. Finally, add the chopped dates and diced apples. The mixture is now ready.

← Butter a cake tin and pour in the prepared mixture. Sprinkle the crushed pistachios and hazelnuts on top and bake for 40 minutes.

For presentation: Remove the cake from the oven and allow it to cool before unmolding. Dust with powdered sugar and enjoy!

LEVEL:
JAFFA APPRENTICE

INGREDIENTS
1 cup (150 g) dates
3 apples
¼ cup (30 g) whole hazelnuts
¼ cup (30 g) pistachios
¾ cups (180 g) butter at room temperature
⅔ cups (150 g) sugar
4 eggs
½ cup (100 ml) cream
1 ½ cups (180 g) flour
2 ⅔ tbsp (20 g) cornstarch
1 sachet baking powder
1 cup (100 g) hazelnut powder
Icing sugar

Serves **4** - Preparation time: **20 MIN** - Cooking time: **6 H**

According to Dr. Ford, in Westworld, it's essential that the scenario offered to the newcomers allows them to get a glimpse of what they might become if they played the game to the hilt. And that means leaving no stone unturned, including the contents of the plates! Here's a recipe that could be served at Mariposa to give newcomers the real taste of the Far West!

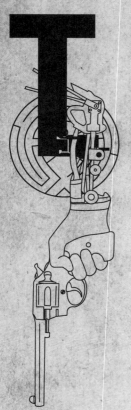

THE EASY TRIGGER

PULLED PORK WITH SPICES AND SWEET POTATO PURÉE

↜ Preheat your oven to 150°C (gas mark 5). Don't arm yourself with a gun, but with patience, as this recipe requires a long cooking time.

↜ Start by preparing the marinade for the meat. Peel and finely chop the garlic and onions, then place them in a mixing bowl. Add the ketchup, cider vinegar, mustard, maple syrup, Worcestershire sauce, paprika, cumin, Tabasco, and fresh thyme. Sprinkle with a good pinch of salt and pepper. Mix all the ingredients together until you achieve a nice, homogeneous marinade. Dip the whole pork shoulder in the marinade.

↜ Pour the marinade-coated pork into an ovenproof dish. Cover and bake for at least 6 hours; the goal is to cook the meat for an extended period to significantly tenderize it.

↜ After 5 hours and 20 minutes of cooking, begin preparing your two-potato mashed potatoes: peel the potatoes and sweet potatoes, then cut them into chunks. Place them in a saucepan, add sparkling water, and bring to a boil.

↜ Cook for 15 to 20 minutes until the vegetables have softened, then drain. Transfer them to a mixing bowl, add the butter, and, using a fork or potato masher, mash the vegetables, leaving some nice chunks. Set it aside while dealing with the pork.

↜ Remove the meat from the oven; it should be tender and well-flavored. Place it on a cutting board and, using a fork, shred it into fine pieces. Then mix the shredded pork with the remaining sauce in the dish and serve. Enjoy your meal!

For presentation: Place two leaves of lettuce on each plate and garnish them with portions of marinated meat. Serve alongside mashed potatoes and a glass of brandy.

LEVEL:
BUDDING COWBOY

INGREDIENTS

FOR PORK
2 garlic cloves
2 large yellow onions
1 ⅓ cups (300 ml) ketchup
1 cup (250 ml) cider vinegar
1 tbsp. mustard
1 tbsp. maple syrup
1 tbsp. Worcestershire sauce
1 tsp. paprika
1 tsp. cumin
2 drops of Tabasco
3 sprigs of fresh thyme
Salt and pepper
2.2 pounds (1 kg) pork shoulder

FOR PUREE
1 pound (500 g) mashed potatoes
½ pound (200 g) sweet potato
6 cups (1.5 l) sparkling water
5 ½ tbsp (75 g) butter
Salt
Pepper

8 fresh lettuce leaves

Serves **4** - Preparation: **20 MIN** · Cooking time: **1 H**

What better way to thank your fellow man than by cooking him a plate of spiced abbey tomatoes. They make all the difference, as Pastor Book used to say: "A man can live on rations until Judgment Day, as long as he has rosemary." Here's a recipe inspired by Earth-That-Was.

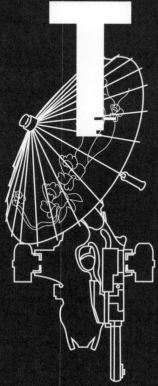

TOMATOES À LA BOOK
BAKED TOMATOES, ROSEMARY, AND CANTONESE RICE

← Preheat your oven to 180°C (gas mark 6).

← Begin by preparing the vegetables: rinse the tomatoes and slice them into 3 mm-thick slices. Peel the onions and thinly slice them. Peel the garlic and finely chop it.

← In an ovenproof sauté pan, heat a generous drizzle of olive oil over medium heat. Add the chopped garlic and sauté for 2 minutes, stirring well. Incorporate the onion and sauté for an additional 2 minutes, seasoning with a pinch of salt, pepper, and sugar.

← Meanwhile, prepare the Cantonese rice to accompany the tomatoes. Clean and chop the spring onions, reserving the green parts for the garnish. Crack the eggs into a bowl, add the milk, and season to taste. Whisk the mixture for a few moments.

← In a frying pan, heat a drizzle of olive oil and pour in the beaten eggs. Cook over medium heat, stirring with a wooden spatula. Once the eggs are cooked, add the rice to the hot pan and pour in the soy sauce. Mix thoroughly and set it aside, off the heat.

For presentation: serve a generous portion of tomatoes alongside the Cantonese rice. Garnish each plate with a few spring onions, including their greens. 让我们吃！

LEVEL:
BEGINNER SMUGGLER

INGREDIENTS

FOR TOMATOES
8 tomatoes
4 green tomatoes
2 onions
2 garlic cloves
Olive oil
1 pinch of sugar
1 tbsp (5 g) Espelette pepper
1 ½ tbsp (5 g) ground chili
4 sprigs rosemary
2 sprigs thyme

FOR CANTONESE RICE
¾ cups (200 g) cooked round rice
2 spring onions
4 eggs
3 ½ tbsp (50 ml) milk
3 ½ tbsp (50 ml) soy sauce
Olive oil
Salt
Pepper

HUBOT'S MEATBALLS

SWEDISH MEATBALLS

LEVEL:
HUBOT

INGREDIENTS

FOR MEATBALLS
2 potatoes
1 onion
4 tbsp (30 g) breadcrumbs
3 tbsp. heavy cream
½ pound (250 g) ground beef
½ pound (250 g) minced pork
1 egg
Flour
1 knob butter
Salt
Pepper

FOR SAUCE
1 beef stock cube
2 tbsp. soy sauce
1 cup (100 ml) crème fraîche
½ tbsp. cornstarch
Salt
Pepper

To step into the hubot (human-robot) Bea's kitchen for a few minutes and prepare some of Roger's favorite dumplings, you'll first need to cook the potatoes. Peel them, place them in a pan of cold water, and bring it to a boil. Reduce the heat and cook for approximately 30 minutes. To check for doneness, insert a knife blade into a potato. If the knife pierces easily, the potato is cooked.

Next, finely chop the onion. Mash the potatoes with a fork and combine them with the chopped onion, breadcrumbs, and cream. Add the beef, pork, and egg. Season with salt and pepper, then mix until the mixture is smooth.

Sprinkle a little flour onto a plate. Shape about a dozen meatballs by hand and coat them with flour.

In a knob of butter, fry the meatballs for 10 minutes. Set them aside.

Now, proceed to prepare the sauce. Place the beef stock cube in a pan of hot water. Once the cube completely dissolves, pour the stock into the previously used hot pan to cook the meatballs. Add the soy sauce. Retrieve the liquid and strain it through a sieve. Combine the liquid with the cream. Add the cornstarch, salt, and pepper. Mix well.

For presentation: Arrange 4 meatballs on each plate and drizzle them with the cream sauce. To complement the dish, serve the meatballs with tomato beans, following Bea's style.

For **8 BISCUITS** - Preparation time: **10 MIN** - Cooking time: **15 MIN**

The Dalek invaders are impossible to resist. Impossible for everyone except the Doctor, who is never short of cunning and daring when it comes to fighting these galactic tin cans. This recipe could well save your life in the future...

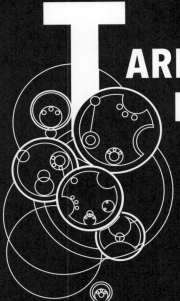

TARDIS AUTODESTRUCTION BISCUIT

HOMEMADE JAMMIE DODGERS

LEVEL:
APPRENTICE TIME LORD

INGREDIENTS

*1 cup (150 g) flour
1 ½ cups (100 g) almond powder
⅔ cups (100 g) powdered sugar
1 sachet vanilla sugar
1 sachet baking powder
⅔ cups (150 g) butter
1 egg
7 tbsp (100 ml) milk
Strawberry jam
Powdered sugar*

❮ Start by preheating your oven to 180°C (gas mark 6). If you don't have an oven, you can use the Tardis reactor, which also works.

❮ Prepare the cookie mix: pour the flour, almond powder, sugar, vanilla sugar, and baking powder into a mixing bowl. Mix well, then make a well in the center.

❮ Melt the butter in a bain-marie or microwave oven. Set aside for a few moments.

❮ Break the egg into the dry mixture well and start mixing. Add the melted butter, then the milk. Mix and knead until you obtain a homogeneous dough.

❮ Lightly flour your work surface and roll out the dough to a thickness of 2 mm. Using a 5 cm diameter biscuit cutter, cut out 16 biscuits. Make a small circle in the center of half the biscuits, using a paring knife or a small 1 cm-diameter biscuit cutter. Place all the biscuits on a baking sheet lined with parchment paper. Bake for 15 minutes.

❮ Remove the biscuits from the oven as soon as they seem firm and start to brown. Leave them to cool on the baking sheet and garnish them when they have completely cooled.

❮ To complete the process, assemble the biscuits: fill the biscuits without a "hole" in the center with strawberry jam. Place the "open-heart" biscuits on top. Sprinkle them with powdered sugar and savor the flavors.

GERONIMOOOO !

For **4 BURGERS** - Preparation time: **30 MIN** - Cooking time: **15 MIN**

The sun rises over Sunnydale, which has survived another few hours of apocalypse from the Hellmouth. It would seem that the Slayer, entrusted with her millennial duty, has watched over all humanity once again this night. As for you, as you emerge from the Bronze, you discover both daylight and the flashing neon lights of the Doublemeat Palace. A young blonde woman with a wry smile and a determined gaze hands you your order. Automatically, you glance at the badge on her uniform. Buffy. What a funny name.

Doublemeat Veggie Burger

BEETROOT, CARROT, POTATO AND ONION BURGER

🥔 To begin, start by preparing the vegetables. Peel the carrots and potatoes, then cut them into 1 cm cubes (mirepoix). Boil them in a saucepan of salted water for 15 minutes once it returns to a boil. Drain and set aside. Cube the beetroot and set it aside as well.

🥔 Finely chop the red onion after peeling it. Remove the garlic germ and chop the garlic finely. All the ingredients are ready; the only remaining step is to blend them. *Be cautious not to leave a finger in the mixture...*

🥔 Combine diced carrots, potatoes, beetroots, red onion, garlic, coriander, chickpeas, and kidney beans in a mixing bowl. Drizzle with olive oil and lightly mash the vegetables with a fork or potato masher for a few seconds. The goal is to retain chunkiness, creating a vegetable mash rather than a complete purée.

🥔 Introduce the whole egg, breadcrumbs, and season with salt and pepper to taste. Gently incorporate these elements, ensuring not to over-crush the mixture. With the vegetable base ready, proceed to shape them: form 4 balls from the vegetable mixture and flatten them with the palm of your hand. Set them aside for a moment.

🥔 In a skillet over medium heat, add a drizzle of olive oil. *If aiming for an exact replication of the Doublemeat Palace recipe, beef fat could be used*, though it's not recommended.

🥔 Once the pan is hot, place the 4 vegetable steaks in it and brown them for 3 minutes on each side. Then, transfer them onto a sheet of kitchen paper.

🥔 Toast your burger buns in the pan, slightly increasing the heat. Let the buns warm and brown for 2 to 3 minutes. Simultaneously, rinse the tomatoes and slice them into thick, juicy slices.

Assemble your Doublemeat Veggie Burgers. Spread Dijon mustard on the inside of the buns, add 1 slice of cheddar, 2 slices of tomato, 2 pickle slices, 1 veggie steak, and finally, a few mesclun leaves. Complete by placing the bun caps on each burger. Enjoy... *and don't forget to take a burger back to your Watcher!*

LEVEL:
KILLER APPRENTICE

INGREDIENTS

FOR VEGGIE STEAKS
*1 large carrot
2 agria potatoes
1 cooked beetroot
1 red onion
1 garlic clove
10 fresh coriander leaves
½ cup (80 g) cooked chickpeas
½ cup (80 g) cooked kidney beans
Olive oil
1 whole egg
1 tbsp. fine breadcrumbs*

FOR THE REST OF THE RECIPE
*4 sesame burger buns
2 tomatoes
4 tsp. Dijon mustard
8 slices mature cheddar
8 slices pickled gherkins
7 cups (100 g) mesclun
Olive oil
Salt
Pepper*

Serves **4** - Preparation time: **20 MIN** - Cooking: **15 MIN**

If your strange new friend with telekinetic powers likes waffles, why not just make her some yourself?

LEVEN'S WAFFLES
TRADITIONAL WAFFLES WITH CRANBERRY COULIS

Start by separating the egg whites from the yolks in two mixing bowls. Add the salt to the egg whites and beat until stiff. Set aside.

Add the sugar to the yolks and mix to whiten the mixture. Stir in the flour and baking powder, then gradually add the egg whites, without breaking them up.

Next, pour in the milk, orange blossom and melted butter: using a whisk, incorporate all the ingredients until the mixture is smooth and lump-free.

Let the waffle batter rest for a few minutes at room temperature, then prepare the cranberry coulis.

Place the fresh cranberries in a saucepan, pour in the juice and bring to a gentle boil for 2 minutes. Add the maple syrup. Set aside off the heat.

Now you're ready to cook your waffles. Heat a waffle iron and pour some batter into each impression. Leave to heat for 3 to 5 minutes, depending on the desired texture. Alternatively, pour the batter into pre-buttered waffle molds and bake for 15 minutes at 200°C (Gas mark. 6-7).

Dressing: there's no need to waste too much time dressing the waffles - *you've probably got a game of Dungeons & Demogorgons to finish off with your friends, haven't you?* Simply pour a little coulis over each waffle, sprinkle with powdered sugar and enjoy...

Is there something wrong with the fuses? What is that strange light?

LEVEL:
PALADIN LEVEL 1

INGREDIENTS

FOR WAFFLES
2 whole eggs
1 pinch of salt
⅓ cup (70 g) sugar
2 cups (250 g) sifted flour
1 sachet baking powder
3 ½ tbsp (500 ml) milk
1 ½ tbsp (20 ml) orange blossom
⅓ cup (80 g) melted butter

FOR THE CRANBERRY COULIS
1 ½ cups (150 g) fresh cranberries
⅔ cup (150 ml) organic cranberry juice
2 tbsp. maple syrup
5 tsp (20 g) powdered sugar

For **10 COOKIES** - Preparation time: **10 MIN** - Standing time: **2 H** - Cooking time: **20 MIN**

As the world has ended and you've fallen prey to the undead, don't hesitate to seek calm and safety in Alexandria! This is the recipe that Carol, a newcomer to the community, prepares for the survivors every day...

AROL'S COOKIES
CHOCOLATE CHIP COOKIES

LEVEL:
BEGINNER SURVIVOR

INGREDIENTS

1 ½ cups (200 g) flour
2 sachets baking powder
1 tsp. cornstarch
1 pinch of salt
¾ cup (170 g) semi-salted butter
½ cup (100 g) sugar
⅔ cup (150 g) brown sugar
1 whole egg + 1 yolk
¾ cup (120 g) chocolate chips

To reproduce these little bites of heaven, mix flour, yeast, cornstarch and salt in a mixing bowl.

In a second bowl, mix the softened butter, sugar and brown sugar by hand. Add the whole egg and yolk and knead again.

Mix the two mixtures by hand and add the chocolate chips. Your cookie dough is now ready. Set aside in the fridge for at least 2 hours.

Preheat oven to 180°C (gas mark 6). Remove the dough from the fridge and shape into ten large balls. Place them on a baking sheet lined with parchment paper. Remember to space them well apart, as they will spread when cooked. Bake for 15 to 20 minutes. Remove the cookies from the oven and leave to rest on a wire rack for 10 minutes. Enjoy!

For **10 MUFFINS** - Preparation time: **10 MIN** - Cooking time: **20 MIN**

CONSTANCE'S WELCOME GIFT
CHOCOLATE MUFFINS WITH CRYSTALLIZED VIOLETS

LEVEL:
DESPERATE HOUSEWIFE

INGREDIENTS

2 eggs
1 cup (170 g) sugar
1 cup (150 g) dark chocolate
¾ cup (180 g) butter
1 ½ cups (200 g) flour
1 sachet baking powder
½ cup (150 ml) milk
½ cup (100 g) chocolate chips
A few crystallized violets
or violet sugar

Preheat oven to 180°C (gas mark 6).

To create muffins as generous as Constance's, begin by whisking the eggs and sugar in a mixing bowl until the mixture lightens and becomes fluffy. Set it aside.

Using a double boiler, melt the chocolate and butter together. Fold this mixture into the egg-sugar blend. Then add the flour and baking powder, mixing until it forms a smooth paste. Gradually pour in the milk while continuing to stir. Finally, gently fold in the chocolate chips. Your muffins are now ready to bake.

Prepare the muffin molds by greasing them and pouring in the batter. Bake for 20 minutes. Once the muffins are fully cooked, you can decorate them with a few crystallized violets, mimicking Constance's style. *However, bear in mind that Constance's method involves her daughter, Addie, spitting into the preparation before adding a few drops of ipecac syrup… Steps to forget if you want to stay on good terms with your friends!*

For **20 CREPES** - Preparation time: **10 MIN** - Standing time: **1 H** - Cooking time: **30 MIN**

As his son can attest, it's not easy to keep a constant eye on Walter Bishop, with his tendency to do as he pleases - rather strangely, it has to be said. Perhaps you can capture his attention by asking him to make you his famous laboratory pancakes, regressive and gourmet to perfection!

WALTER BISHOP'S GUILTY PLEASURE
TRADITIONAL BISHOP-STYLE PANCAKES

LEVEL:
*QUANTUM PHYSICS
STUDENT, FIRST YEAR*

INGREDIENTS

FOR PANCAKE BATTER
*4 cups (500 g) flour
½ cup (100 g) sugar
1 sachet vanilla sugar
6 eggs
1 ½ cups (400 ml)
semi-skimmed milk
5 ½ tbsp (20 g) semi-salted butter
1 pinch of salt
3 ½ tbsp (50 ml) blonde beer
Sunflower oil*

FOR THE BLUEBERRY COULIS
*5 cups (1 kg) fresh blueberries
2 tsp. powdered sugar*

To make light pancakes, combine flour, sugar, vanilla sugar, eggs, and milk in a mixing bowl. Whisk vigorously until any lumps dissolve. If the dough is too thick, you can thin it out with a little water. Add the melted butter and salt and mix again.

Your pancake batter is almost ready. Place the bowl in the fridge for at least 1 hour.

Meanwhile, prepare the coulis. Pour the blueberries and sugar into a large saucepan and heat over medium heat, uncovered, for 20 minutes, stirring regularly. Leave to cool.

Take the pancake batter out of the fridge and add the beer to make it lighter. If Walter Bishop is accustomed to heating his pancakes in a frying pan over a Bunsen burner, we'd advise you to stick to your usual hotplates instead.

Pour the oil onto absorbent paper and lightly oil the pan. Light the griddle over medium heat. When the pan is hot, pour in a ladleful of batter and swirl until it fills the pan. Wait 30 seconds. and flip the pancake, then place it on a plate. Continue in this way until the mixing bowl is empty.

To serve: stack the pancakes on a plate as you would pancakes, and pour over a dollop of blueberry coulis. Enjoy!

Serves **6** - Preparation time: **20 MIN** - Cooking time: **30 MIN**

Ah, if only it were possible to live a simple life, without demons or violence! If only everything could be summed up in a slice of apple pie! A slice of pie you could finally enjoy with your brother or Castiel! Why not bake it yourself?

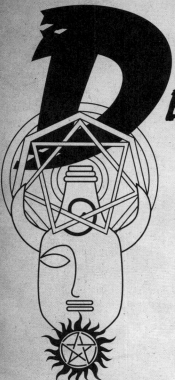

DEAN'S APPLE PIE

APPLE, PEAR, AND MAPLE SYRUP TART

Preheat your oven to 200°C (Gas mark 6-7).

Start by preparing the pasta: roll out the first layer and cut into strips. Place on a sheet of parchment paper and refrigerate. Line a thick cake tin with the other dough. Using the tip of a fork, prick the bottom of the pastry and place the tin in the fridge while you prepare the filling.

Prepare the fruit: peel the apples and pears. Remove the cores and cut into strips. Place the slices in a large mixing bowl and sprinkle with lemon juice. Add cinnamon, nutmeg, sugar, and maple syrup. Using a wooden spoon, stir the mixture until smooth. Set aside for a few moments.

Melt the butter in a saucepan over low heat or in the microwave. Pour over the fruit mixture and mix well. Set aside for a few moments. Remove the tin from the fridge and fill with the fruit mixture. Cover with the strips of shortcrust pastry.

Now all you need to do is make the finitions: using a brush, brush the pastry strips with the beaten egg yolk. Sprinkle with brown sugar and bake for 30 minutes.

Serving suggestions: enjoy a generous slice of warm tart with a scoop of vanilla ice cream. *Mmmh, that smell! Doesn't it remind you of Bobby's wife's pies? Or maybe this pie from a small town in Indiana...*

LEVEL:
APPRENTICE HUNTER

INGREDIENTS

2 store-bought or homemade shortcrust pastries (recipe page 40)
1 pound (500 g) granny smith apples
1 pound (500 g) willams or conference pears
Juice of 1 lemon
⅔ tsp (2 g) cinnamon
⅔ tsp (2 g) ground nutmeg
4 tbsp (50 g) caster sugar
2 tbsp. maple syrup
1 ¾ tbsp (25 g) butter
1 egg yolk
A few pinches of brown sugar

John H Watson

POP CULTURE WE BE

THE BIG BANG THEORY

After a long day of research at Caltech spent enduring the taunts of that pesky Kripke and comparing the size of his telescope with those of his colleagues, what could be better than stopping off at the Cheesecake Factory to enjoy a BBQ burger (with sauce, bacon, and cheese on the side, yes, that'll be all)?

THE BBQ BURGER
BURGER WITH BARBECUE SAUCE

❀ *Make sure your hands are perfectly clean before preparing the dish. Check again. Wash your hands again if in doubt.*

❀ Now prepare the buns. Mix the flour, butter, egg and 250 ml warm water in a bowl. Knead for 5 minutes. Add the salt, sugar and baking powder and knead again for 10 minutes. Your dough is now ready, but you'll need to leave it to develop. Cover the bowl with a damp cloth and leave to rest for 1 hour.

❀ Preheat the oven to 200°C (gas mark 6-7). At this stage, the dough should have doubled in volume, which is scientific. Knead it again on a floured surface. Divide the dough into 4 balls. Melt a knob of butter in a container in the microwave oven and, using a brush, coat the dough balls with the melted butter. Bake for 20 minutes, until the buns are golden brown. Remove from the oven and cut in half.

❀ Prepare the burger. Start by peeling and chopping the onion. Chop up the jalapeño. Combine the minced meat, onion, jalapeño, and egg in a bowl. Mix by hand and shape into burgers.

❀ Move on to cooking the filling. Pan-fry the bacon for a few minutes until completely caramelized. Pan-fry the burgers in the bacon fat until cooked to desired doneness. Finally, brown the inside of the buns in the pan with the bacon fat.

Assembly: preheat oven to 150°C (gas mark 5). Assemble the bun, burger, bacon, and cheese. Place the burgers in the oven for a few minutes to melt the cheese. Remove the burgers from the oven and add the salad and barbecue sauce. For perfect absorption of this delicious burger, you can also eat all its components separately. *And remember, the burger is only served on Tuesday evenings!*

LEVEL:
APPRENTICE COOK

INGREDIENTS

FOR BUNS
3 ⅓ cups (420 g) flour
2 tbsp (30 g) and a knob
of butter
1 egg
1 pinch of salt
4 tbsp (50 g) sugar
1 tbsp (16 g) baker's yeast

FOR TOPPINGS
1 red onion
1 jalapeño pepper
2 ⅓ cups (600 g) minced meat
1 egg
8 slices cheddar cheese
8 slices bacon
4 lettuce leaves
Barbecue sauce

Serves **6** - Preparation time: **30 MIN** - Standing time: **30 MIN** - Cooking time: **1 H 45**

Federal Bureau of Investigation
Bureau File Number 10131013
SWEET POTATO PIE CASE
Field Office Criminal Investigative
and Administrative File

MULDER'S SWEET POTATO PIE

SWEET POTATO PIE

☸ Start by cooking the sweet potatoes. Brush them and place them in a pan of cold water, whole with their skins. Bring to the boil, then reduce the heat to medium and leave for 40 minutes, until the core of the sweet potatoes become tender.

☸ While the sweet potatoes are cooking, prepare a shortcrust pastry. Cut the softened butter into cubes. Mix the flour, butter, and salt in a bowl by hand until the dough has a sandy texture. Gradually add 50 ml of water while continuing to mix, and form the dough into a ball. Cover the bowl with a damp cloth and leave the dough to rest for 30 minutes.

☸ After this time, roll out the dough to a thickness of 3 mm on a floured work surface, using a rolling pin. Line a tart tin and prick the pastry with a fork.

☸ Preheat oven to 180°C (gas mark 6). Peel the sweet potatoes. Mash them in an ovenproof bowl. Melt the butter in the microwave and add to the mashed sweet potatoes. Mix well.

☸ Add sugar, milk, eggs, nutmeg, cinnamon, and vanilla extract.

☸ Mix with an electric mixer until smooth.

☸ Pour the mixture over the shortcrust pastry and bake for 1 hour. You can check doneness by pricking a knife into the center of the tart. If the blade comes out clean, the tart is cooked through.

Serving suggestions: serve generous portions on a plate and top with a dollop of whipped cream. *Just the thing to boost your spirits before setting off on your next investigation!*

LEVEL:
SPECIAL AGENT TRAINEE

INGREDIENTS

FOR THE SHORTCRUST
PASTRY
½ cup (100 g) soft butter
1 ½ cup (200 g) flour
3 ⅓ tbsp (50 ml) water
Salt

FOR FILLINGS
1 pound (500 g) sweet potatoes
½ cup (125 g) soft butter
1 cup (200 g) powdered sugar
½ cup (120 ml) milk
2 eggs
½ tsp. ground nutmeg
½ tsp. powdered cinnamon
1 tsp. vanilla extract
Whipped cream

Serves **6** - Preparation time: **30 MIN** - Cooking time: **2 H**

Life isn't always easy when you're running a funeral home as a family; in fact, for the Fishers, the dead sometimes seem to be easier to deal with than the living! Fortunately, for all those situations where it's good manners to invite someone to dinner and offer quality social interaction, a good moussaka should put everyone on the same page...

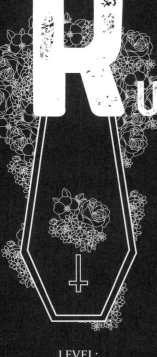

RUTH'S MOUSSAKA
TRADITIONAL MOUSSAKA

❀ Start by preparing the vegetables: peel and finely chop the onion. Set aside for a few moments, then move on to the tomatoes. Peel and dice the tomatoes (place in boiling water for a few moments, then peel). Set aside.

❀ Peel the potatoes and cut into thin slices. Finally, wash and slice the eggplants and drain with a little salt. Now that your vegetables are ready, you can move on to the next stage of preparation.

❀ Heat a drizzle of olive oil in a frying pan over medium heat. Add the onion and sweat for a few minutes without browning. Add the tomatoes, cinnamon, honey, and meat. Simmer for a few moments over medium heat. When the meat starts to cook, add the tomato coulis. Add salt and pepper to taste. Cover and reduce for 30 minutes.

❀ Meanwhile, preheat the oven to 180°C (gas mark 6). Drizzle a little olive oil over the bottom of a gratin dish and place the potato slices on top. Place in the oven for 10 to 15 minutes, until lightly browned.

❀ While the potatoes are browning, place the eggplant slices in a frying pan for a few minutes with a drizzle of olive oil, to lightly toast them. Remove the gratin dish from the oven. Turn the oven up to 200°C (Gas mark 6-7). Assemble the moussaka. Add half the meat mixture to the potatoes, then arrange half the eggplants on top. Add the other half of the meat and the remaining eggplants. Set aside.

❀ Now it's time to prepare the béchamel sauce. Melt the butter in a small saucepan over medium heat, then add the flour and milk very slowly, stirring constantly. Add a little nutmeg. Simmer, stirring, until the béchamel thickens. Pour the sauce over the top of the dish and bake for 1 hour.

Presentation: remove the dish from the oven and serve portions on a plate with green salad.

LEVEL:
AMATEUR MORTICIAN

INGREDIENTS

1 onion
5 tomatoes
6 potatoes
2 large eggplants
1 pinch of salt
1 tsp. cinnamon
1 tbsp. honey
2 ⅓ cups (600 g) ground beef
1 cup (250 g) tomato coulis
Olive oil
Salt
Pepper

FOR THE BÉCHAMEL SAUCE
1 ½ (20 g) butter
4 level tablespoons flour
1 ½ cup (350 ml) milk
Nutmeg

Green salad

You've just arrived at Albuquerque's Los Pollos Hermanos restaurant and are waiting for your date. Mmmh... why not try some of those mouth-watering chicken wings they serve here?

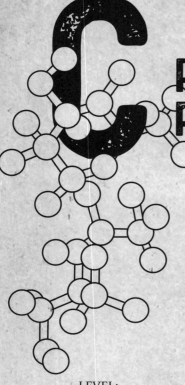

CRISPY CHICKEN BY POLLOS HERMANOS
CRISPY CHICKEN WINGS

✿ Start by preparing your chicken wings: sprinkle them with salt and paprika before setting aside in the fridge.

✿ Move on to the buttermilk, a preparation much used by the Anglo-Saxons, which will add a crispy texture to your chicken wings: pour the milk, yoghurt and a dash of white vinegar or lemon juice into a mixing bowl. The idea is to add an acid to lower the pH of the milk and make it curdle, i.e. coagulate the casein, the main protein in milk. Set aside for 10 minutes, until the mixture thickens.

✿ Prepare the ingredients for the breadcrumbs: pour the flour, chili powder (Jessie's bloody secret ingredient) and Parmesan powder into a mixing bowl. Mix well and set aside. In a separate bowl, beat the eggs and set aside. Pour the Panko breadcrumbs into a bowl. You're now ready to bread your chicken wings.

✿ Start by pouring a little buttermilk into the flour mixture. Then follow the steps in this order: dip the chicken wings in the buttermilk, then in the flour, then in the eggs, then in the breadcrumbs, then in the eggs again, and finally in the breadcrumbs again. Your wings are ready to go in the pan!

✿ Prepare kitchen paper. Pour the frying oil into a casserole dish and heat to 170°C (use a cooking thermometer to check the temperature). Dip the breaded chicken wings in the hot oil for between 5 and 8 minutes, then, using tongs, place them on sheets of kitchen paper as they cook. Sponge off excess oil and serve.

Serving suggestions: you can enjoy these chicken wings with a little homemade barbecue sauce and fresh coriander. *By any chance, isn't the restaurant manager your man?...*

LEVEL:
POLLITO

INGREDIENTS

*12 trimmed chicken wings
(prepared by your butcher)
½ tbsp (10 g) fine salt
4 tsp (10 g) paprika*

FOR BUTTERMILK
*¾ cup (200 ml) whole milk
1 whole yoghurt
1 ⅓ tbsp (20 ml) white vinegar
or lemon juice
2 cups (500 ml) frying oil*

FOR BREADING
*2 ½ cups (300 g) flour
9 tbsp (30 g) chili powder
2 tbsp (30 g) parmesan
powder
2 eggs
Panko breadcrumbs
Barbecue sauce
Fresh coriander*

THE BEST KEY LIME PIE IN TOWN
AMERICAN KEY LIME PIE

LEVEL:
NOVICE SERIAL KILLER

INGREDIENTS

FOR PASTRY
4 cups (340 g) speculoos cookies
3 tbsp (35 g) caster sugar
¾ cup (180 g) semi-salted butter
1 egg

FOR THE FILLING
2 egg whites
1 ⅓ tbsp (10 g) powdered sugar
4 egg yolks
1 can sweetened condensed milk
4 limes
Whipped cream

❁ Start by preparing the dough for the key lime pie: blend the speculoos cookies to a powder. Melt the butter in a microwave oven. Mix the speculoos powder with the sugar, melted butter and egg. Spread the batter in a removable-bottom mold, pressing well with a tablespoon to obtain a smooth, even surface. Refrigerate for at least 1 hour (or freeze for 15 minutes).

❁ Meanwhile, prepare the whipped cream: start by beating the egg whites with the powdered sugar in a mixing bowl. Beat until stiff. To check their firmness, carefully invert the bowl. If the whites do not fall, they are sufficiently stiff.

❁ In a second bowl, combine the egg yolks and sweetened condensed milk. Zest the limes and add the grated zest to the bowl. Mix again. Squeeze the limes and add the juice to the mixture. Mix again until smooth.

❁ Add a third of the egg whites, without breaking them, to the lemon mixture and mix with a spatula. Add the rest of the egg whites and continue mixing until well incorporated.

❁ Preheat oven to 180°C (gas mark 6). Remove the springform pan from the fridge (or freezer) and pour the mixture over the dough. Bake for around 20 minutes, until firm. To check this, you can, for example, insert the blade of a knife into the center of the tart. If the blade comes out clean, the pastry is well done. You can also gently shake the tin and check that the center of the tart is not softer than the edges, which generally cook faster.

❁ Remove the tart from the oven and place on a wire rack until cool.

❁ Place the key lime pie in a cool place for at least 2 hours.

Serving suggestions: for those with a sweet tooth, add a little whipped cream just before serving to give it a creamy texture.

Serves **4** - Preparation time: **35 MIN** - Cooking time: **1 H 30**

A tidy kitchen, labelled cuts of meat, classical music in the background, and you are plunged into the elegantly macabre world of Dr Hannibal Lecter. For this osso-buco recipe, we have taken the liberty of replacing Michelle Volcason's leg with a traditional veal shank. And it is best to stick to this less tasty version if you don't want to get into trouble with the authorities...

DR. LECTER'S OSSO-BUCO

MILANESE VEAL OSSO-BUCO

LEVEL:
SEASONED CANNIBAL

INGREDIENTS

2 tomatoes
4 carrots
3 small stalks celery
2 onions
5 garlic cloves
½ cup (100 ml) olive oil
1 ¾ pounds (800 g)
veal shank
Flour
½ cup (150 ml) dry white wine
1 cup (300 ml) chicken stock
(see page 94)
Salt
Pepper
Zest of 1 orange
3 anchovy fillets
2 tsp. capers

❄ Start by preparing the vegetables: wash and prune the tomatoes (place in boiling water for a few moments, then peel). Remove seeds and chop coarsely. Set aside.

❄ Peel the carrots and cut into mirepoix (1 cm cubes). Rinse the celery and cut into large cubes. Peel and chop the onions. Finally, chop the garlic. Set all the vegetables aside.

❄ Now it's time to prepare the meat. In a pressure cooker, pour in a good drizzle of olive oil and heat over medium heat. Singe the veal shanks (coat with flour) and brown on all sides.

❄ Remove the meat from the pan and set aside for a few moments. Place the vegetables in the meat juices and sauté for 5 minutes until lightly browned. Return the meat to the pan and pour in the white wine. Reduce the sauce by half over a low heat for 20 minutes. Add the chicken stock to the remaining sauce. Add salt and pepper to taste, then close the pressure cooker. Simmer under pressure for 1 hour.

❄ While the meat is simmering, prepare the final garnish. Zest the orange and plunge the zest into a pan of boiling water. Rinse and drain. Chop the anchovy fillets.

❄ In a bowl, combine the orange zest, anchovies, and capers. Set aside for a few moments, until you remove the pan from the heat and let off the steam. You can already smell that special aroma. Open the pressure cooker and pour in the orange-anchovy-caper mixture. Cover and simmer for a further 10 minutes.

Serving: serve on attractive white china plates with a glass of red wine.

Serves **4** - Preparation time: **20 MIN** - Cooking time: **1 H**

When they weren't planning their next raid to the West and neighboring territories and placing their fate in Odin's hands, the Vikings were a people of fishermen, farmers, and craftsmen. Alongside roasted meats, fresh goat's cheeses and golden beers, here's what might have sated Jarl Lothbrok and his followers at the feast table of Kattegat Hall.

KATTEGAT LAND-SEA STEW

TROUT, NETTLE, AND BOILED VEGETABLES

✿ Start by preparing the vegetables: peel and chop the onion and garlic cloves. Peel and slice the carrots. Peel the potatoes and cut into quarters. Peel the turnip and cut into eight equal pieces. Rinse the spinach leaves. Finally, crush the pink berries and pepper. Lightly salt the trout fillets and set aside in the fridge.

✿ Place the crushed berries and pepper in a stewpot over medium heat and roast them for a few moments until their fragrance fills the stewpot. Add the butter, onion, and garlic. Cook until they begin to brown. Add the carrots, potatoes, turnip, and spinach leaves. Season to taste and sauté for 5 minutes over medium heat. Pour in the fish stock, add the bouquet garni and parsley. Cover and simmer for 40 minutes.

✿ When the vegetables have finished cooking, add the nettle leaves and trout fillets to the casserole. Remove from the heat and cook in the broth, covered, for 10 minutes. Serve, *and don't forget to honor the gods!*

LEVEL:
GYDA

INGREDIENTS

1 yellow onion
2 garlic cloves
4 carrots
4 potatoes
1 golden turnip
12 fresh spinach leaves
4 pink berries
4 black peppercorns
3 ½ tbsp (50 g) butter
8 cups (2 l) fish stock
1 bouquet garni
½ bunch parsley
A few nettle leaves
4 trout fillets
Salt
Pepper

SHERLOCK

Serves 4 - Preparation time: **15 MIN** - Standing time: **30 MIN** - Cooking time: **30 MIN**

There are simple pleasures in life: putting up shelves, driving your landlady mad or operating on a patient with an open heart during a game of Doctor Maboul... But we can add to this list the pleasure of a good fish and chips, and particularly that of the Marylebone Road shop.

MARYLEBONE ROAD FISH AND CHIPS
TRADITIONAL FISH AND CHIPS

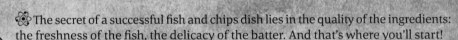

The secret of a successful fish and chips dish lies in the quality of the ingredients: the freshness of the fish, the delicacy of the batter. And that's where you'll start!

Preheat oven to 180°C (gas mark 6). Start by separating the egg whites from the yolks: pour the yolks into one mixing bowl and the whites into another. Add a pinch of salt to the whites and, using a hand whisk or electric mixer, beat until stiff. Set aside.

Add the flour and beer to the egg yolks. Still using a whisk, mix these elements until you obtain a homogeneous paste. Fold the egg whites into the remaining mixture. Set the batter aside in the fridge for 30 minutes.

While they're resting, prepare the fries: brush the potatoes under a trickle of water. Dry them and cut into matchsticks. Mix them with the olive oil in a bowl. Lay them flat on a baking tray lined with baking paper and bake for 25 minutes, until crisp and cooked through.

Finally, prepare the fish. In a deep fryer or casserole, heat the sunflower oil to 170°C (check with a cooking thermometer). Prepare a large plate lined with kitchen paper. Cut the cod into large, even pieces and dip them into the fritter batter. Place them in the hot oil for 5 to 6 minutes, then place them on the paper towel. If necessary, and depending on your fat tolerance level, use additional sheets of kitchen paper to remove excess oil.

To serve: *you can serve these fish and chips in newspaper... but above all, you must serve them with a homemade tartar sauce (see page 94). So British.*

LEVEL:
AMATEUR DETECTIVE

INGREDIENTS

1 ⅓ pounds (600 g) french fries
1 ⅓ pounds (600 g) cod fillets
4 cups (1 l) sunflower oil
3 tbsp. olive oil

FOR THE BATTER
2 whole eggs
1 ½ cups (200 g) flour
¾ cup (200 ml) blonde beer, or dark beer
1 pinch of salt

FANTASY

Serves **6** - Preparation time: **20 MIN** - Standing time: **30 MIN** - Cooking time: **35 MIN**

DOUBLE R DINER CHERRY PIE
CHERRY AND CHOCOLATE PIE

✳ Preheat your oven to 180°C (gas mark 6). Start by preparing the sweet almond paste: pour the flour, sugar, and almond powder into a bowl. Set aside for a few moments.

✳ Beat the eggs in a bowl and set aside. Dice the butter and add to the dry mixture in the bowl. Knead with your fingertips to incorporate the butter and obtain a sandy texture. Add the beaten eggs and continue kneading to incorporate them. The dough is ready when it forms a homogeneous ball between your fingers: wrap it in cling film and set aside in the fridge for 30 minutes.

✳ While the dough is resting, prepare the cherry filling: wash, stem and pit the cherries. Place them in a saucepan and add the sugar, cornstarch, and lemon juice. Mix well and simmer for 20 minutes over medium heat, stirring regularly to prevent sticking. Set aside in the pan off the heat.

✳ Take up the dough ball once the 30-minute rest period has elapsed. Flour your work surface, remove two-thirds of the dough, and roll it out using a rolling pin. Line a high-sided tart tin and, using a fork, prick the pastry all over the surface, not forgetting the edges.

✳ Pour the cherry compote over the dough and spread it evenly with the back of a tablespoon. Grate the dark chocolate over the compote and set aside for a few moments.

✳ Still on a floured work surface, roll out the remaining dough and cut into neat strips. In a bowl, mix the egg yolk with a few drops of black coffee (or water if you don't like coffee), then brush over the dough strips. Arrange the strips on the surface of the cherry compote in a checkerboard pattern, for example, and bake for 35 minutes.

Serving suggestions: serve warm or cold portions of this cherry pie to your guests. *Don't forget to save at least 2 slices for Special Agent Cooper. Be sure to serve them with a cup of coffee as black as a moonless night - that's how he prefers it.*

LEVEL:
FBI TRAINEE

INGREDIENTS

FOR THE SWEET ALMOND PASTRY
3 cups (400 g) flour
½ cup (100 g) sugar
¾ cup (75 g) almond powder
2 whole eggs
1 cup (200 g) soft butter
at room temperature

FOR FILLINGS
6 ¼ cups (1 kg) fresh cherries
(Or 5 cups (800 g) pitted cherries)
2 ⅓ cups (20 g) cornstarch
½ cup (100 g) sugar
3 ½ tbsp (50 ml) lemon juice
2 ⅓ tbsp (25 g) dark chocolate
1 egg yolk
1 ⅓ tbsp (20 ml) black coffee

Serves **6** - Preparation time: **30 MIN** - Cooking time: **30 MIN**

KING JOFFREY'S DEADLY PIE
PIGEON AND MUSHROOM PIE

LEVEL:
KING'S BUFFOON

INGREDIENTS

*¾ pound (400 g) butcher's
pigeon meat
½ pound (250 g) fresh button
mushrooms
⅔ cup (80 g) lardons
¾ cup (200 ml) chicken stock
(see page 94)
¾ cup (200 ml) light cream
2 tsp (5 g) curry powder
2 homemade or store-bought
shortcrust pastries
(see page 40)
1 egg yolk
Salt
Pepper*

✳ Preheat oven to 200°C (gas mark 6-7). Start by preparing the stuffing: dice the pigeon meat using a sharp, toothless knife. Set aside. Wash and peel the mushrooms. Cut into thin strips. Set aside.

✳ Heat a frying pan over low heat. Sauté the lardons for a few minutes, until they begin to brown. Then add the diced pigeon and mushrooms without adding any fat: they'll cook in the fat of the lardons. Simmer for 5 minutes, then deglaze with chicken stock and simmer until the stock has evaporated. The stuffing is almost ready. *Don't waste any time, King Joffrey wouldn't tolerate a delay to his wedding ceremony*. Add the cream and curry powder. Season with salt and pepper. Set aside off the heat.

✳ Next, assemble the pie. Line a tart tin with parchment paper. Line the tin with the first piece of shortcrust pastry. Pour in the pigeon mixture.

✳ Close the pie with the second shortcrust pastry. Lightly moisten your fingers and seal the edges of the two pastries. Don't hesitate to cut the second pastry if it's too big and keep the excess.

✳ Feeling like an artist? At your own risk, but in this case, form a ball from the excess dough, then roll it out with a rolling pin. Using a sharp knife, draw leaves, flowers or any other pattern that inspires you and add them to the cobbler. Brush the top of the cobbler with egg yolk to help the pastry brown in the oven.

✳ Make a small cross in the center of the pastry with a knife. This will allow the steam to escape, so that the cobbler won't be soft when it comes out of the oven. Bake for 30 minutes.

To serve: Serve this pretty pie in generous portions, using a knife or sword. This recipe is ideal for all types of festivities, such as a large banquet...

Serves **6** - Preparation time: **30 MIN** - Cooking time: **30 MIN**

Not sure you'll be getting back on a plane any time soon! For now, you'll have to survive, and to do that, you'll have to remember what your fisherman father taught you long ago. Ah, if only you had all the ingredients you need to make that old Korean recipe for grilled fish...

J IN FISH

GRILLED MACKEREL, MANGO, AND LEMON

LEVEL:
NEW ROBINSON

INGREDIENTS

⅔ cup (150 ml) gochujang
sauce
⅔ cup (150 ml) soy sauce
6 ¾ tbsp (100 ml) mirin
1 tsp (5 g) freshly chopped
ginger
2 tsp (5 g) pepper
1 small bunch of coriander
2 whole, cleaned mackerel
Olive oil
2 almost ripe mangoes
1 lime

✳ First, you'll need to make the marinade that will coat the fish as it cooks. To do this, you'd need to take a mixing bowl and pour in the gochujang sauce, soy sauce, mirin, ginger, pepper, and a few coriander leaves. Then the marinade would be ready, and you could move on to the fish: *if you hadn't just caught it in your filets, you should make sure that* the mackerel is quite firm and its eyes bright, which are the signs of its early freshness.

✳ Then you'd dip your shucked and gutted mackerel in the marinade, so that they're well covered, and their flesh is coated. Set them aside for a few moments.

✳ Pour a drizzle of olive oil into a frying pan or grill and heat over medium heat. Place the mackerel in the pan and cook for 5 minutes on each side.

✳ While they're cooking, you could prepare your mangoes: you'd need to peel them and, using a paring knife, scoop out the flesh around their core, then cut them into cubes before setting them aside.

✳ In a small frying pan, heat a drizzle of olive oil over medium heat. Add the diced mangoes and sprinkle with lime juice. Cook for 2 minutes over medium heat before serving with fresh coriander leaves.

If only you could taste those marinated fish and mangoes... Instead, you're lost on a desert island, forced to share sea urchins with a hairy young man who really doesn't understand anything...

Serves **4** - Preparation time: **20 MIN** - Cooking time: **45 MIN**

Between two viewings of Full Contact, Capheus never says no to a little dish cooked by his mother, Chichi, because it's a well-known fact that trouble looks lighter on a full stomach. In fact, Chichi specializes in sukuma and ugali, two typical Kenyan dishes.

Sukuma and Ugali from Chichi
Braised Kale with Tomato and Cornbread

✳ Start by preparing the Sukuma: peel and chop the onion, slice the kale, and dice the tomatoes. Set aside.

✳ Heat a drizzle of sunflower oil over medium heat in a heavy-bottomed saucepan. Add the onion, kale, and tomatoes, and cook for 5 minutes before gently basting with the vegetable stock. Add salt and pepper to taste. Bring to the boil and reduce heat. Simmer for 30 minutes.

✳ While the Sukuma is simmering, prepare the ugali, which is a typical starchy food in Kenyan cuisine. To do this, nothing could be simpler: pour 1 l of water into a saucepan and add the fine salt before bringing to the boil. When the water boils, pour in the corn flour. Over low heat, using a wooden spatula, stir until the mixture becomes quite sticky. Remove the saucepan from the heat and scrape down the sides to collect all the mixture, stirring until any lumps disappear. The ugali is ready!

To serve: *pour the Sukuma into a large shallow dish and spread evenly. Place the ugali in the center of the dish, on top of the kale. May Jean-Claude's strength protect you!*

LEVEL:
VAN DAMME APPRENTICE

INGREDIENTS

FOR SUKUMA
1 onion
2 bunches of kale
2 tomatoes
Sunflower oil
*¾ cup (200 ml) vegetable stock
(see page 94)*
Salt
Pepper

FOR UGALI (CORNBREAD)
½ tsp. table salt
3 ¾ cups (500 g) cornflour

Serves **6** (5 CAPTIVES AND 1 TORTURER) - Preparation time: **20 MIN** - Cooking time: **2 H 15**

Here's a recipe for borscht as young Nina might have learned it from her father, in Russia, before Kathun took her eyes and gave her back her life, before she became Prairie Johnson, before she became The OA...

Borsch Azarov
Russian beetroot soup

✳ Start by preparing the vegetables: peel the potatoes and cut them into mirepoix (1 cm cubes). Set aside. Rinse and chop the cabbage. Peel and grate the carrots and beetroot. Peel the onion and garlic and chop finely. Rinse and dice the tomatoes. *Make sure none of your guests are allergic to them... yet.* Set all the vegetables aside.

✳ To prepare the meat and stock, cut the beef and pork into nice, even pieces. Pour the olive oil and butter into a casserole dish and heat over medium-high heat. Place the pieces of meat in the casserole and sear them on all sides. Season to taste, add the marrow bone and top up with water. Cover and simmer for 30 minutes from the first boil.

✳ Meanwhile, heat a drizzle of olive oil in a frying pan over medium heat. Add the garlic, onion, carrots, beetroot, and diced tomatoes. Season to taste, cover and reduce for 15 minutes. Add the wine vinegar and reduce for a few more minutes.

✳ Meanwhile, add the potatoes and chopped cabbage to the casserole with the meat. Cover and cook for 30 minutes before adding the pan-fried vegetables and bouquet garni. Cover and simmer for a further 1 hour.

Presentation: Serve the borscht as soon as it's ready, because, as Mr. Azarov used to say, it's never as good as when it's just been cooked. Serve in 6 bowls, with 1 tsp. crème fraîche and a sprinkling of fresh parsley.

LEVEL:
APPRENTICE DANCER

INGREDIENTS

6 floury potatoes
1 small white cabbage
2 carrots
1 large raw beetroot
1 yellow onion
1 garlic clove
3 tomatoes
1 ¾ pound (800 g) trimmed roast beef
¾ pound (400 g) trimmed pork filet
Olive oil
1 ½ tbsp (20 g) butter
1 marrow bone
3 ⅓ tbsp (50 ml) wine vinegar
1 bouquet garni
4 tsp. crème fraîche
1 small bunch of fresh parsley
Salt
Pepper

Serves **6** - Preparation: **5 MIN** - Cooking: **10 MIN** - Standing: **5 MIN**

"Once upon a time, there was a princess who was as white as snow, as ruddy as blood and as black-haired as ebony [...] and Snow White was her name because of this. When she reached adolescence, the wicked Queen of the kingdom, jealous of her beauty, wanted to stuff her with a beautiful ruddy apple. Snow White longed for this beautiful apple, but no sooner had the first bite been in her mouth than she fell dead to the floor."

The Brothers Grimm

But plese make sure, the apple you're about to prepare will not be fatal, but only have a marvellous taste...

THE POISONED APPLE
LOVE APPLE

LEVEL:
PRINCE CHARMING BEGINNER

INGREDIENTS

2 cups (250 g) powdered sugar
2 ½ tbsp (50 g) glucose
6 wooden skewers
6 Pink Lady apples
1 ½ tbsp (20 g) butter
5 drops red food coloring

✳ To make an appetizing red apple, start by making a caramel. There's nothing too complicated about this preparation, but it does require a little care and attention.

✳ To obtain a syrupy, coating caramel, pour 120 ml of water into a saucepan. Add the sugar and glucose. Heat until the caramel reaches 150°C (gas mark 5). If you don't have a cooking thermometer, leave the caramel to cook for 10 minutes after boiling, always keeping an eye on the pan to make sure it doesn't burn.

✳ While the caramel is being prepared, wash the apples and skewer them.

✳ Remove the pan from the heat and add the butter. Pour in the red colorant. Don't hesitate to add a few drops if you feel your caramel isn't red enough. Mix vigorously with a spatula.

✳ Immediately dip the apples one by one into the caramel until they are completely covered.

✳ Place the apples, wooden spike side up, on a sheet of baking paper or a smooth plate, until the caramel hardens and looks like a lollipop, *so delicious that your worst enemies won't be able to resist it...*

Serves **6** - Preparation: **30 MIN** - Marinade: **12 H** - Standing time: **5 MIN** - Cooking time: **1 H 30**

Demon-hunting between the Halliwell sisters is all well and good, but sometimes it's just as nice to get together for a meal like a normal family, to unwind after another battle with Barbas or a harrowing trip down memory lane. After all, every family has its own routine and its own Book of Shad... of recipes.

PIPER'S COQ AU VIN
TRADITIONAL COQ AU VIN

* Start by mixing the wine, oil, bouquet garni and pressed garlic in a large container to create a fragrant marinade. Detail the rooster: pare the legs, breast, and wings. Place in the marinade for at least 12 hours.

* Once the meat has been infused with these multiple flavors, you can continue preparing the coq au vin.

* Peel and chop the white onions. Set aside. Place the lardons in a large pot of cold water. Bring to the boil and cook for 2 minutes. The idea is to reduce the fat and impurities in the lardons. Drain and set aside for a few moments.

* Heat 1 tbsp. oil and half the butter in a casserole dish. Add the lardons and chopped onions and cook them until golden brown. Drain and remove excess fat using kitchen paper.

* Now it's time to assemble all the ingredients in a pot, *as if you were preparing a decoction from the Book of Shadows.* In a small saucepan, heat the brandy. Pour the brew into the casserole, flambé it all... *Time for some incantations, don't you think?*

* Add the red wine marinade to the pot and bring slowly to the boil. Cover and simmer for 1 hour.

* While this powerful dish is simmering, peel and slice the button mushrooms. Melt a knob of butter in a frying pan and sauté the mushrooms for 5 to 10 minutes, until all the water has evaporated. Add them to the pan. Simmer for a further 20 minutes.

* Now it's time for the finishing touch! Melt the remaining butter in the microwave. Mix with the flour and a ladleful of red wine marinade. Pour the resulting mixture into the casserole and cook for a further 5 minutes, until the sauce thickens slightly. Enjoy!

Serve this sharing dish directly in a casserole on the table and let your guests help themselves. *Bon appétit and may the Power of Three set you free!*

LEVEL:
WITCH'S APPRENTICE

INGREDIENTS

4 cups (1 l) red wine
½ cup (100 ml) + 1 tbsp. olive oil
1 bouquet garni
2 garlic cloves
1 rooster, approx. 4 ½ pounds
(2.5 kg)
20 small white onions
½ pound (200 g) lardons
⅓ cup (80 g) butter
¾ cup (200 ml) cognac
2 ½ cups (200 g) button
mushrooms
1 tbsp. flour
Salt
Pepper

HIGHLANDER

Long gone are the days when you enjoyed the life in your little village of Glenfinnan, the days when you flirted with Debra Campbell, the days before your first Quickening. Why not cook a traditional Scottish recipe - haggis - that you could share with Connor? To prepare and, above all, cook this dish, you need patience and time. It's not as if you're short of it...

Glenfinnan Haggis
Stuffed Sheep's Belly with Braised Root Vegetables

✳ Start by preparing the stuffing for the haggis: peel and finely chop the onions and shallots. In a small pan of boiling water, blanch them for 5 minutes, then drain. Chop the parsley and set aside.

✳ Bring a large volume of salted water to the boil and plunge the mutton frass into it. Leave to cook for 1 hour and 30 minutes once it has returned to the boil, then drain. Remove impurities and chop with a knife. Set aside for a few moments.

✳ Heat a skillet over medium heat and brown the oat flakes for a few minutes until crisp. Stir in the chopped flank steak, ground beef, onions, shallots, parsley, cayenne pepper and nutmeg. Season with salt and pepper, then add 250 ml of vegetable stock. Cook over medium heat until the stock is reduced. Gather the stuffing into a ball.

✳ Stuff two-thirds of the lamb's belly with the stuffing, squeeze out the air and seal with kitchen string. Using a small needle, pierce the belly in two or three places, so that it doesn't burst during cooking.

✳ Bring a pot of water to the boil and immerse the belly in it. Cover and simmer for 3 hours and 30 minutes.

✳ After 2 hours and 30 minutes of cooking, prepare the vegetables that will accompany this delicious haggis: peel parsnips, rutabagas, potatoes, and turnips. Cut them into mirepoix (1 cm cubes). Heat a frying pan and pour in the olive oil and butter. Once the butter has melted, add the vegetable cubes, season to taste and sauté for 2 minutes. Add the remaining vegetable stock and simmer over low heat for 15 minutes.

Serve this sharing dish as soon as the haggis is cooked. Drain the haggis and slit the belly to reveal the richly flavored stuffing. Serve with a generous portion of braised vegetables.

LEVEL:
BUDDING HIGHLANDER

INGREDIENTS

*3 onions
2 shallots
1 small bunch of fresh parsley
2 pounds (1 kg) mutton offal /
tripe (liver, heart, lung)
4 cups (500 g) oat flakes
½ pound (200 g) ground beef
2 tsp (5 g) cayenne pepper
1 ½ tsp (5 g) nutmeg
Salt
Pepper
1 ½ cup (400 ml) vegetable stock
(see page 94)
1 mutton belly, washed
and rinsed
2 parsnips
6 small rutabagas
6 Charlotte potatoes
6 fresh turnips
Olive oil
1 ½ tbsp (20 g) butter*

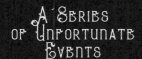

Serves **4** - Preparation time: **15 MIN** - Cooking time: **15 MIN + 7 MIN**

You don't want to try this recipe. If I were a thoughtful narrator, I'd warn you that you shouldn't even consider reading this page. Or even these lines. In short, don't go any further in this introduction. Ah, you're the stubborn type. Either you think you're smarter than everyone else. Or maybe you're Count Olaf. All right, then...

SPAGHETTI PUTTANESCA
SPAGHETTI WITH TOMATO SAUCE, ANCHOVIES, AND OLIVES

LEVEL:
CHILDREN'S MENU
(unless your name is Baudelaire, in which case the recipe may lack crunch)

INGREDIENTS

4 tomatoes
2 garlic cloves
1 cup (80 g) desalted anchovies
½ cup (80 g) pitted black and green olives
½ bunch parsley
2 ⅔ tbsp (20 g) capers
1 chili
2 tbsp. olive oil
1 ½ tbsp (20 g) butter
3 tbsp (40 g) coarse salt
4 cups (400 g) spaghetti
Salt
Pepper

✳ Start by preparing the various ingredients for the puttanesca sauce. Wash and prune the tomatoes (place in boiling water for a few moments). Drain and plunge them immediately into a cool water bath. Remove their stalks and peel them. Finally, crush them and set aside.

✳ Peel the garlic and place in a mortar or vegetable chopper. Add the desalted anchovies and vigorously crush these two ingredients (just imagine it's the nauseating side of the count you're crushing, it'll give you a real workout). Halve the olives and chop the parsley. Finely chop the capers. Remove the seeds from the chilies and chop finely. Now that all the ingredients are ready, all you need to do is start cooking.

✳ Pour the olive oil and butter into a casserole dish. Melt the butter over medium heat, then sauté the garlic-anchovy mixture for 4 minutes, stirring constantly: you can already smell the Mediterranean fragrance and the sunshine outside your window.

✳ Add the olives, capers, chili pepper and parsley and sauté for a further 2 minutes, stirring constantly, before adding the crushed tomatoes. Add salt and pepper to taste, then leave the sauce to simmer, covered, for around ten minutes. The perfect time to cook your spaghetti!

✳ Pour 4 l of water and the coarse salt into a large pot. Bring to the boil and immerse the spaghetti in the water for 7 minutes. Keep an eye on the pasta, which should be cooked al dente, but firm to the bite. Drain the pasta and add it immediately to the puttanesca sauce, where it will finish cooking for a few seconds. Then you can move on to the dining room to serve!

Preparation time: **30 MIN** · Cooking time: **10 MIN** · Standing time: **30 MIN**

"A new restaurant is opening its doors in our beloved Papen County. If you enjoy home cooking with gourmet flavors or are simply looking for a warm atmosphere in which to dine, the Pie Maker and his smiling employees Chuck and Olive will welcome you to the Pie Hole with pies so delicious you may remember them until the day you die!"

Advertisement published in The Papen County Picayune, n° 2208

Chuck's Strawberry and Honey Delight Tarlets

Strawberry and Honey Tartlets

✳ Preheat oven to 180°C (gas mark 6).

✳ Start by making the honey shortcrust dough: combine the flour, salt, and softened butter in a mixing bowl. *Make sure you're as delicate as Chuck would be* and mix until you get a sandy texture.

✳ In a separate bowl, whisk the egg yolks with the sugar. Add 50 ml water. *Climb onto the roof of your house to collect honey from your favorite bees* and add it to the mixture with 1 pinch of salt. Knead well and shape into a ball, dividing it into 8 mini dough pieces.

✳ Line tartlet tins with parchment paper and place a few ceramic balls (or dried beans) on top to prevent the pastry from sticking during baking. Bake for 5 minutes.

✳ Now that your tart dough is baking, you can move on to the pastry cream. Preparation is a two-step process. First, bring the milk and vanilla sugar to the boil in a saucepan. Keep a close eye on the cooking process, as the milk can quickly boil over!

✳ In a large bowl, whisk together the egg and sugar. Add the flour. Pour the hot milk over this mixture, stirring vigorously. Pour the mixture into the saucepan, stirring constantly until it boils. Remove the pan from the heat and leave to cool. Now you've made a delicious custard in just a few minutes.

To Serve: Spread a little custard on each tart base. Rinse the strawberries under running water and hull. Cut the strawberries into thin strips and arrange them in a rosette on the surface of the pastry cream. Finally, dust each tartlet with a little powdered sugar. Your strawberry and honey tarts are ready to enjoy. *No doubt your culinary talent will make Ned jealous!*

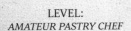

LEVEL:
AMATEUR PASTRY CHEF

INGREDIENTS

FOR THE SHORTCRUST PASTRY
2 cups (250 g) flour
½ cup (125 g) butter
2 egg yolks
3 tbsp (40 g) sugar
1 tbsp. honey
1 pinch of salt

FOR THE PASTRY CREAM
1 cup (250 ml) milk
1 sachet vanilla sugar
1 egg
2 ½ tbsp (30 g) sugar
4 tbsp (30 g) flour

FOR FILLINGS
½ pound (250 g) strawberries
⅓ cup (40 g) powdered sugar

ALIAS INVESTIGATION

JESSICA JONES
485 W. 46TH ST
NEW YORK, NY 10036

www.aliasinvestigation.com

SUPERPOWERS

X

X

九

DAREDEVIL

For **1 OMELETTE** - Preparation time: **5 MIN** - Cooking time: **5 MIN**

Here's a quick and easy recipe for an omelette as served in the world's finest restaurants. To make it perfectly, you'll need calm, concentration, and patience, so slip into your most comfortable silk pajamas and put on a cello suite in the background.

KINGPIN'S OMELETTE
FOLDED OMELETTE WITH SNIPPED CHIVES

◆ Start by breaking 3 eggs into a mixing bowl. Pour in the milk, salt, and pepper. Using a whisk, beat the eggs for a few moments (stop before they get frothy). Set aside.

◆ Heat a frying pan over medium heat and place the butter on the surface to melt slowly, without ever coloring it. Once the butter has melted, pour in the beaten eggs. Still over medium heat, cook for 3 to 5 minutes, gently stirring the surface. The eggs should never stick to the surface, so that the cooking process is smoother, and the heart of the omelette stays soft.

◆ The challenge in this recipe is to make an omelette that folds in on itself. *Here, we prepare it as the Kingpin would, simply, soberly, with finesse.* Feel free to add some elements to your taste like ham, cheese or diced fresh tomatoes, for example, before folding the omelette.

◆ To do this, you can start by using a spatula to fold one half of the omelette over the other. Then modify your grip, taking the pan handle from underneath and inverting the omelette directly onto the plate.

Dressing: wash the chive stems under a trickle of water and dry. Using a paring knife, chop them. Place the fresh chives on the surface of the omelette and enjoy.

LEVEL:
JUSTICIER

INGREDIENTS

3 eggs
3 ⅓ tbsp (50 ml) whole or semi-skimmed milk
1 pinch of salt
1 pinch of pepper
1 ½ tbsp (20 g) soft butter

10 sprigs of fresh chives

Good old Harvey Bullock has never been much of a cook, or even a gourmet, but he's not averse to forsaking his glass of beer for a few moments when he gets the chance to indulge in a sweet Irish treat. It's even said to put him in a good mood...

GCPD BULLOCK DOUGHNUTS

GUINNESS AND CHERRY DOUGHNUTS

LEVEL:
GCPD DETECTIVE

INGREDIENTS

3 cups (400 g) flour
⅓ cup (60 g) sugar
¾ tsp (5 g) salt
2 eggs
1 ½ tbsp (20 g) baking yeast
½ cup (150 ml) milk at room temperature
8 tsp (40 ml) Guinness
⅓ cup (80 g) butter, diced
1 cup (250 ml) cherry confiture
1 ½ cup (400 ml) frying oil
Castor sugar

◆ For this recipe, we'll be using a food processor fitted with a dough hook. However, you can knead the dough by hand if you don't have a food processor: it will just take a little longer.

◆ Pour the flour, sugar, and salt into the bowl of a food processor and mix well. Create a well.

◆ In a separate bowl, beat the eggs until frothy. Pour the beaten eggs, baking powder, milk, and Guinness into the center of the well. Knead the dough for 5 minutes on medium speed, until it comes away from the bowl. Add the butter and knead for a further 5 minutes.

◆ Using a horn or spatula, scoop out the contents of the bowl and shape the dough into a ball. Set aside for 1 hour in a bowl covered with cling film or a clean tea towel. This hour's rest will help the dough to "grow": the yeast does its job, and the dough rises.

◆ Once the dough is well risen, place it on a floured work surface. Press it down with your fist to release the gas slightly (*a bit like Bullock would do with the heel of his shoe on the face of an inconvenient suspect*). Next, cut the dough into 10 thick pieces: with each piece, form a small ball in the palm of your hand. Place 1 tsp. cherry jam on top and close the ball on itself. Then, using a rolling pin, roll out each ball of dough to a thickness of 2 to 2.5 cm.

◆ In a high-sided frying pan, heat the frying oil to 180°C (use a cooking thermometer to check the temperature).

◆ Dip the fritters in the oil bath, 4 minutes on each side. Once nicely colored, remove and place on paper towels.

Dressing: sprinkle your cherry fritters with castor sugar and enjoy them at your leisure. *Enjoy the moment, let your colleagues do the dirty work... Ah, the good life...*

For **4 BENTOS** - Preparation time: **40 MIN** - Cooking time: **20 MIN**

Ah, if only life were monotonous. If only Ando and your colleagues believed you when you told them you possessed the power to alter the space-time continuum... Why not have lunch now and try to move the hand of your clock back just one tiny second?

YAMAGATO BENTÒ

WASABI TUNA ONIGIRI. BREADED TOFU. STUFFED SHIITAKE. AND CUCUMBER-WAKAME SALAD

LEVEL:
HERO APPRENTICE

INGREDIENTS

*2 cups (400 g) Japonica
or Arborio round rice
½ cup (100 ml) rice vinegar
3 tbsp (40 g) castor sugar
1 tsp (5 g) salt
⅓ pound (150 g) cooked tuna
(canned tuna)
2 tbsp. mayonnaise
A hint of wasabi
4 small, dried nori leaves*

WASABI TUNA ONIGIRI

 Start by preparing the onigiri: rinse the rice several times until the rinse water is clear. Pour into a saucepan with 500 ml of water and bring to the boil. Cook for 12 minutes on a very low heat, then leave the rice to rest, covered, off the heat for 10 minutes.

Meanwhile, pour the vinegar, sugar, and salt into a saucepan. Melt the sugar and salt over a low heat, but do not bring to the boil. Set aside.

Collect the rice and place in a large bowl. Pour over the vinegar/salt-sugar mixture and mix well with a wooden spatula, so as not to crush the rice grains. If you can, use a fan to cool the rice while you stir in the vinegar. Your vinegared rice is now ready. Set aside for a few moments under a damp cloth.

In a small bowl, crumble the tuna, add the mayonnaise and wasabi, and mix well. To assemble the onigiri, place a generous amount of rice in the palm of your hand (or in an onigiri mold). In the center, add 1 tsp. of tuna-mayonnaise-wasabi. Close with a little rice and press lightly with your hands to mold the onigiri. Accompany each onigiri with a small nori leaf.

BREADED TOFU

INGREDIENTS

3 ½ tbsp (50 ml) soy sauce
3 ½ tbsp (50 ml) mirin
1 clove garlic, minced
2 ½ tsp (5 g) fresh ginger, minced
½ cup (120 g) tofu
2 ¼ tbsp (20 g) black sesame seeds
2 ½ tbsp (20 g) Panko breadcrumbs
Frying oil

◆ To prepare the tofu sticks, start by making a small marinade. Pour the soy sauce, mirin, garlic, and ginger into a mixing bowl. Mix well and add the tofu. Refrigerate for 20 minutes.

◆ Meanwhile, prepare the breadcrumbs: mix the black sesame seeds and Panko breadcrumbs on a plate. Drain the tofu and cut into sticks. Place them in the breadcrumbs so that the tofu is well covered.

◆ Pour the frying oil into a frying pan. Heat to 170°C (you can check the temperature with a cooking thermometer), then plunge the sticks into the hot oil for 1 minute and 30 seconds. Drain as you go on a sheet of kitchen paper. The breaded tofu is ready.

STUFFED SHIITAKE

INGREDIENTS

12 shiitake
1 shallot
2 tbsp. soy sauce
Juice of 1 lemon
2 tbsp. black sesame oil

◆ Preheat the oven to 200°C (gas mark 6-7).

◆ Clean the mushrooms. Chop 4 of them finely. Peel and finely chop the shallot. Place the chopped mushrooms and shallot in a bowl. Pour in the soy sauce and lemon juice and mix well. Core the remaining 8 mushrooms and top with the chopped mixture.

◆ Place on a baking sheet lined with parchment paper. Brush the shiitake mushrooms with black sesame oil and bake for 10 minutes. The mushrooms are ready.

CUCUMBER-WAKAME SALAD

INGREDIENTS

½ cup (10 g) dried wakame
1 cucumber
2 tbsp. mirin
2 tbsp. soy sauce
1 tsp. black sesame oil
Black sesame seeds

◆ To prepare the cucumber-wakame salad, rehydrate the wakame in a bowl of water for a few minutes. Meanwhile, prepare the cucumber. Peel and slice finely. Set aside.

◆ Make a vinaigrette by mixing the mirin, soy sauce and black sesame oil in a bowl. Add the chopped cucumbers and wakame. Sprinkle with black sesame seeds.

◆ Your bentos are ready, *YATTAAAAA*!

Serves 4 - Preparation time: **15 MIN** - Cooking time: **20 MIN**

We don't know if young Clark Kent's superpowers allow him to cook with greater ease (beating eggs without cramping his arm...) or speed (cooking eggs with laser vision, for example), but here's a recipe he won't mind preparing for his parents or friends in Smallville, the creamed corn capital of the world!

KANSAS-STYLE CREAMED CORN
CREAMED CORN AND BACON WITH SPINACH

LEVEL:
BUDDING FARMER

INGREDIENTS

FOR THE CREAMED CORN
*1 cup (280 g) corn kernels
1 cup (250 ml) heavy cream
2 tbsp. castor sugar
1 tsp. salt
¼ tsp. ground black pepper
2 tbsp (30 g) butter
1 cup (250 ml) whole milk
2 tbsp. flour
½ cup (50 g) grated Parmesan
cheese*

FOR THE SPINACH ROLL
*1 ¾ pound (800 g) fresh spinach
1 onion
3 ½ tbsp (50 g) semi-salted
butter
Pepper
8 round slices of bacon*

 To prepare this dish, pour the corn kernels, cream, sugar, salt, pepper, and butter into a frying pan. Heat over low heat for 5 minutes.

 In a separate bowl, whisk together the whole milk and flour, then pour the mixture into the frying pan. Sauté over medium heat until thickened. Remove the pan from the heat and add the grated Parmesan. Stir until the cheese has melted.

 Next, prepare a wilted spinach, the star vegetable of Kansas cuisine. Wash and spin the fresh spinach and remove the leaf stalks. Peel and chop the onion. Melt the butter in a frying pan and add the onion until lightly browned. Add the spinach and cover for 2 minutes. After this time, the spinach should have reduced considerably in volume. Remove the lid and stir. Season with pepper and set aside.

 On a clean work surface, lay out the bacon slices. Add a spoonful of spinach to the center of each slice and roll into a cylinder.

 Brown the spinach bacon rolls in the pan, without adding any fat.

Serve on a plate with 1 generous slice of creamed corn and 2 rolls per person.

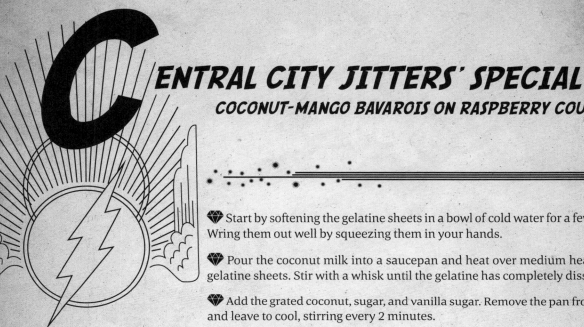

CENTRAL CITY JITTERS' SPECIAL
COCONUT-MANGO BAVAROIS ON RASPBERRY COULIS

LEVEL:
SUPERHEROES

INGREDIENTS

FOR BARAVOIS
2 sheets of gelatine
¾ cup (200 ml) coconut milk
⅓ cup (30 g) grated coconut
3 ½ tsp (15 g) sugar
1 sachet vanilla sugar
¾ cup (200 ml) crème fraîche

FOR THE RASPBERRY COULIS
⅔ cup (150 g) sugar
4 cups (500 g) fresh raspberries

FOR MANGO SOUFFLÉ
1 mango
1 tbsp. cane syrup
2 sheets of gelatin

◆ Start by softening the gelatine sheets in a bowl of cold water for a few minutes. Wring them out well by squeezing them in your hands.

◆ Pour the coconut milk into a saucepan and heat over medium heat. Add the gelatine sheets. Stir with a whisk until the gelatine has completely dissolved.

◆ Add the grated coconut, sugar, and vanilla sugar. Remove the pan from the heat and leave to cool, stirring every 2 minutes.

◆ When the coconut cream has cooled, add the crème fraîche fresh from the fridge and whisk vigorously.

◆ Pour the mixture into 4 individual buttered or silicone bavarois molds and chill for 3 hours.

◆ While the bavarois is setting, prepare the raspberry coulis. Pour the sugar into a saucepan with 200 ml water and bring to the boil. Lower the heat and leave to simmer for 5 minutes.

◆ While the syrup is setting, wash the raspberries and place in a blender. Remove the pan from the heat and pour the syrup over the fruit. Blend until smooth. Strain the coulis through a sieve. Set aside.

◆ Prepare the mango jelly. Peel and chop the mango, then blend to a purée. Strain through a sieve to remove the filaments. Add the cane syrup and mix well. Soak the gelatine sheets in a bowl of cold water until softened. Pour the mango purée into a saucepan. Heat over low heat and add the gelatine. Stir until the gelatine has completely dissolved. Leave to cool to room temperature.

Presentation: just before serving the bavarois, cut the mango jelly into 4 Flash éclair toppings. Pour the raspberry coulis into 4 shallow dishes until the bottom is full. Remove the bavarois from the fridge and carefully unmold onto each plate. Place the Flash toppings on each bavarois. *Enjoy in a flash!*

ALIAS INVESTIGATION

JESSICA JONES
485 W. 46TH ST
NEW YORK, NY 10036

www.aliasinvestigations.com

JESSICA JONES

What's been going on? Why is the apartment in such a state? Who trashed the living room? What happened to the glass in the front door? And who left that banana cake lying around on the desk? Before we can find the answers to these questions, we're going to have to pour ourselves a glass of whisky. Mmmh... but where's that bottle?

RUBEN'S BANANA CAKE

BANANA CAKE

LEVEL:
BEGINNER BAKER

INGREDIENTS

2 cups (250 g) flour
¾ cup (160 g) sugar
1 sachet baking powder
½ tsp. baking soda
3 ripe bananas
6 tbsp (85 g) butter
2 tbsp. milk
2 eggs

◆ Preheat oven to 160°C (Gas mark 4-5).

◆ Mix 150 g flour, sugar, baking powder, bicarbonate of soda and peeled and mashed bananas with a fork. Set aside.

◆ Melt the butter in a bowl in the microwave. Add the melted butter and milk to the previous mixture. Whisk vigorously until smooth.

◆ Crack the eggs and add one at a time to the mixture. Mix again. Finally, add the remaining 100 g flour and mix well.

◆ When your banana bread mixture is ready, butter the bottom of a rectangular cake tin and pour in the batter. Bake for 55 minutes, then, without burning yourself, remove the cake from the oven and let it rest for 30 minutes before eating.

Serving suggestions: feel free to enjoy this banana cake straight from the tin, with a glass of rum... *and hope your usual bottle of whisky won't hold it against you.*

Lexicon

B

BOUQUET GARNI
A collection of aromatic herbs tied into small bundles and used as a seasoning. It is generally composed of thyme, bay leaf and a leek leaf.

BROWN
Cook food in a little fat over high heat until colored.

BRUNOISE
Cut vegetables into 2 mm cubes.

C

CAST IRON CASSEROLE
A thick, conductive cast-iron vessel with a heavy lid for even, steaming cooking.

CHOP
To reduce a foodstuff to small pieces using a knife, chopper, or food processor.

CORNSTARCH
Cornstarch is a corn flour used to bind sauces and thicken preparations, as well as in the preparation of cakes.

CRUSHING
Chop and cut food coarsely.

F

FLOUR
Sprinkle flour on a surface to prevent sticking.

G

GLUCOSE
Glucose is a pure carbohydrate produced from cornstarch, in the form of a thick, viscous syrup. In pastry-making, its role is to prevent sugar crystallization, enabling better control when baking macaroons, cakes, caramels and more.

GOCHUJANG
A hot fermented paste of Korean origin made from red pepper, soy, and glutinous rice flour. Available in specialized Asian grocery stores.

J

JALPEÑO PEPPER
Jalapeño is a variety of pepper native to Mexico. Grown all year round, green, or red, Jalapeño is a relatively hot pepper.

K

KATSUOBUSHI
Katsuobushi is a preparation of dried and grated bonito - a fish similar to bluefin tuna. It adds a salty note to the preparations to which it is added. It has a rather poetic way of reacting to heat...

KIKURAGE
White or brown mushroom. Used in Asian cuisine, it is often sold dried. Slightly gelatinous when rehydrated, it accompanies many soups and potions in Chinese and Japanese cuisine.

L

LOWER
Using a rolling pin, roll out the dough on a floured work surface to the desired thickness.

M

MARINADE
A marinade is a liquid, aromatic preparation used to flavour meat, fish, or vegetables.

MATCHA
Matcha is a fine powder of ground green tea. Rich in vitamins and minerals, matcha has many benefits. With its distinctive green color, matcha can be used to flavor and color cream or cakes.

MIREPOIX
Mirepoix is a technique for cutting vegetables into large cubes.

MIRIN
Similar to sake, mirin is a rice vinegar used as a sweet, syrupy condiment for seasoning in Japanese cuisine. It can be found in supermarkets and Asian grocery stores.

MISO

Miso is a paste made by fermenting soybeans, cereals such as wheat, barley or rice, and other ingredients. Very salty and high in protein, miso paste can be used to make broths or other condiments.

MIXING BOWL

Half-sphere-shaped bowl, usually in stainless steel.

MIXTURE

Mixed ingredients.

P

PEEL

Remove the skin from a vegetable using a paring knife or vegetable peeler.

R

RESERVE

Set aside a preparation or food during a recipe for use at a later date.

S

SIMMER

Cook food over low heat.

SOBA

Sobas are Japanese noodles made from buckwheat flour.

SLICE

Cutting vegetables or fruit into thin slices or strips using a knife or mandolin.

SWEAT

Cook vegetables over a low heat to release their flavors without adding color.

W

WHIPPED CREAM

Full cream with more than 30% fat whipped with a whisk or electric mixer until it takes on volume and solidity. If powdered sugar is added during the process, the whipped cream becomes Chantilly cream.

Knives

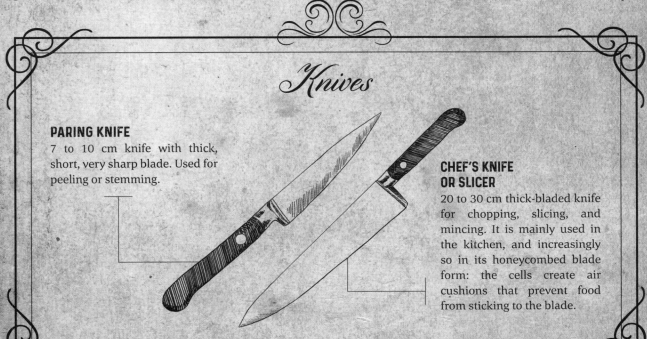

PARING KNIFE

7 to 10 cm knife with thick, short, very sharp blade. Used for peeling or stemming.

CHEF'S KNIFE OR SLICER

20 to 30 cm thick-bladed knife for chopping, slicing, and mincing. It is mainly used in the kitchen, and increasingly so in its honeycombed blade form: the cells create air cushions that prevent food from sticking to the blade.

Tips

VEGETABLE BROTH

Preparation time: **10 MIN** - Cooking time: **2 H** - Standing time: **30 MIN**

INGREDIENTS

4 carrots, diced
1 white leek
1 bouquet garni (1 green leek,
4 parsley stalks, 1 fennel sprig,
1 bay leaf, 1 thyme sprig)
½ stalk of celery

1 onion
1 shallot
8 cups (2 l) water
150 ml white wine
1 star anise
3 cardamoms

Put all the ingredients in a stewpot and simmer, covered, for 2 hours. Leave to stand for 30 minutes off the heat, then strain the stock.

TARTAR SAUCE

INGREDIENTS
SERVES 4
1 onion
2 tbsp. capers
6 gherkins
¼ bunch of parsley
¼ bunch of tarragon
A few sprigs of chives
¼ cup (60 g) homemade mayonnaise
½ stalk of celery

Prepare the vegetables and herbs: peel and cut the onion into small 2 mm cubes (brunoise). Chop the herbs. Set aside.

Mince the capers and gherkins in a blender. Set aside.

Pour the mayonnaise into a mixing bowl. Add the onion, capers and gherkins, then the aromatic herbs.

Mix briskly with a whisk.

CHICKEN STOCK

Preparation time: **20 MIN** - Cooking time: **2 H 15**

INGREDIENTS

2 kg poultry carcass
100 ml grapeseed oil
¼ cup (50 g) soft butter
1 garlic clove
2 shallots
2 l water
1 bouquet garni (thyme and bay
leaves in a green leek leaf)
1 sprig rosemary
2 juniper berries
1 pinch cracked pepper

Crush the poultry carcass and brown in a stewpot with the grapeseed oil and 50 g butter. Stir and simmer over medium heat until the carcass turns a light color. Remove and set aside. Skim the fat from the stewpot, keeping the juices at the bottom. Simmer the garlic and shallots in these juices for just 5 minutes over medium heat. Pour in the water, add the bouquet garni and simmer for 1 hour and 30 minutes. 30 minutes before the end of cooking time, add the rosemary sprig, juniper, and cracked pepper. This infusion will add strength and flavor to your stock. At the end of the 2 hours cooking time, strain the contents of the stewpot to retain only the juice and set aside.

Thanks

Thibaud Villanova

I'd like to say a big thank you to the whole team who've been with me on the Gastronogeek project for nearly 3 years: to Bérengère, my wife, without whom this adventure would have no flavor, thank you for being there and living it all with me. Thanks to Adrien, Satoru, Anna, and Alexis, who help me keep this ship moving forward! Thanks to Mathilde for following me on this stopover dedicated to TV series! Thanks to Soizic and Nicolas for their energy and creativity, and for giving this book such a special polish. Thanks to Julien and Marine for their work on this book, it was a real pleasure to design it with you! Thanks also to Julien Laval, Thomas Olivri, Dominika Roslon, Krystel Maquet, Marie Palot, Lucas Hauchard, Olivier Jalabert, Chahid Tamsamani, for their friendship, help and advice. Thank you to my family and to my father for his cooking lessons, his love of the right gesture and of what's good. Thank you to my sister Laurie, for her invaluable help and great skills as a make-up artist! And thanks to Émilie Pernet for stepping through the looking glass for a photo! Thanks to Samuel and Claude from Pulp Toys, rue Dante in Paris, for supplying and finding many of the fabulous accessories I used for this book. And last but not least, thanks to Catherine Saunier-Talec, Antoine Béon and Anne Vallet of Hachette Editions for the confidence they've shown in me for several years now.

Mathilde Bourge

I'd like to thank my mother, Catherine, for giving me a taste for cooking, and Yohann for being my guinea pig for so many years. Thanks to my father, Hervé, my brothers Arnaud, Guillaume and Alexandre, and my sisters-in-law Gaëlle, Sylvaine and Marion for their support. Thanks to Maïlys, Anne-Cécile, Charlotte, Capucine, and Cécile for always believing in me. Noémie, my cookie tester. But above all, thanks to Thibaud for giving me a chance!

Soizic Chomel de Varagnes and Nicolas Lobbestaël

We'd like to extend our warmest thanks to some of our friends and family, who gave us a helping hand or two in putting together this beautiful book. Thanks to our food lovers: Lorène de Turckheim, Morgane Rey, Arnaud Ziezio. Thanks to Laurence Brun, Julien Luis, Aurélie Ziezio and Charlotte Riesi for the accessories they lent us, enabling us to produce images as close as possible to the series! And above all, a big THANK YOU to Anne and Thibaud for trusting us. But above all thanks to Thibaud for giving me a chance!

MANAGEMENT: Catherine Saunier-Talec

PROJECT MANAGER: Antoine Béon

PROJECT MANAGER: Anne Vallet

EDITORIAL PACKAGING: Gastronogeek SAS

ARTISTIC DIRECTOR: Bérengère Demoncy

DESIGN: Bérengère Demoncy et Julien Escalas

Reviewed by Fabienne Vaslet

PRODUCTION: Isabelle Simon-Bourg

Printed in China by LPP
Published by Titan Books, London, in 2024.

Titan
BOOKS

A division of Titan Publishing Group Ltd
144 Southwark Street
London SE1 0UP
www.titanbooks.com

Find us on Facebook: www.facebook.com/titanbooks
Follow us on X: @TitanBooks

Published by arrangement with Hachette Heroes:
www.hachetteheroes.com

A CIP catalogue record for this title is available from the British Library.
ISBN: 9781835410349
10 9 8 7 6 5 4 3 2 1